Her children rise up and call her blessed;
her husband also, and he praises her:
"Many women have done excellently,
but you surpass them all."

PROVERBS 31:28-29

For Kelly and Rachel,

my two favorite young mamas

a pocketful of
HOPE
for mothers

Robin Jones Gunn

Illustrated by Lauren Lowen

Tyndale House Publishers, Inc., Carol Stream, Illinois

LIVING
EXPRESSIONS™
COLLECTION

Coweta Public Library System
85 Literary Lane
Newnan, GA 30265
770-683-2052
www.cowetapubliclibrary.org

Living Expressions invites you to explore God's Word and express your creativity in ways that are refreshing to the spirit and restorative to the soul.

Visit Tyndale online at www.tyndale.com.

Visit the author's website at www.robingunn.com.

TYNDALE and Tyndale's quill logo are registered trademarks of Tyndale House Publishers, Inc. *Living Expressions* and the Living Expressions logo are trademarks of Tyndale House Publishers, Inc.

A Pocketful of Hope for Mothers

Copyright © 2018 by Robin's Nest Productions, Inc.

Illustrations by Lauren Lowen. Copyright © by Tyndale House Publishers, Inc. All rights reserved.

Cover lettering by Koko Toyama, copyright © 2017 by Tyndale House Publishers, Inc. All rights reserved.

Hand-lettering fonts copyright © by Joanne Marie/Creative Market. All rights reserved.

Designed by Julie Chen

Edited by Janet Kobobel Grant

Published in association with the literary agency of Books & Such Literary Management, 52 Mission Circle, Suite 122, Santa Rosa, CA 95409

For information about special discounts for bulk purchases, please contact Tyndale House Publishers at csresponse@tyndale.com, or call 1-800-323-9400.

ISBN 978-1-4964-2556-0

Printed in China

24   23   22   21   20   19   18
7   6   5   4   3   2   1

Contents

Where the Blue Feathers Hide

My grandmother always kept a treasure or two in the pocket of her apron.

She made her aprons from colorful remnants of summer dresses and stitched them on her olive-green Singer sewing machine. Every apron had a front pocket that went all the way across like a kangaroo pouch.

My memories of her apron pockets seem to revolve around a roll of butterscotch Life Savers I'd almost always find when I slid my eager hand into her pocket. I'd hold up my discovery, and she'd peel back the waxy lining and offer me one of the sweets with a smile. Always with a smile.

One time I found a small pink seashell in her pocket. She told me a tiny creature had once lived inside that shell deep in the ocean. The animal moved out, and its little house tumbled all the way to shore, where she discovered it on a winter morning walk. She bent over and whispered that the shell was mine. I could keep the small wonder.

I clutched that bit of mermaid's loot all afternoon. It spoke to me of worlds beyond my own and marvels yet to experience.

Another treasure I pulled from her pocket was a blue feather. I imagined some wondrous bird dropping the nearly weightless piece of beauty to flutter down, a gift from the sky, for my grandmother to scoop up and tuck into her pocket for me.

Years after my grandma went to heaven, my cousin Cindy sent me some of our grandma's belongings. In the box I found a delicate fan from Korea, a card with a handwritten verse on it, a glittery sweater pin, and one of her aprons. I put the apron on and slipped my hands into the pocket. The only treasure I found was memories. Invisible, but still inspiring.

The apron is, at this very moment, in my kitchen towel drawer. The other gifts are tucked away with one of my grandma's journals. A hobby of hers was collecting witty remarks and poignant quotes along with her favorite Bible verses. She had lovely handwriting and was skilled at making smiley faces every couple of pages.

As I was sorting through my own collection of various stories, prose, and favorite verses for this book, memories of my grandma and her aprons rested warmly in my thoughts. I smiled as I remembered the small treasures she collected and hid in her pocket, waiting for me to find them.

I don't have a roll of Life Savers hidden between these pages for you. You won't find a pink shell or a blue feather to clutch and marvel over. All I have to give you, dear little mama, is words. Sweet words. True words. Words of hope.

You'll find my favorite Bible verses on motherhood along with thoughtful quotes sprinkled throughout the two sections—"Now" and "Then." In the Now section, you'll peer into the thoughts I've shared in talks and through personal letters with young mothers in this generation. My favorite part of the Now section is the journal entries I penned as I watched our grown children welcome their own babies into the world. The Then section contains excerpts from the journals I kept when our two children were young.

Go ahead. Slip your hand into this pocketful of hope, and know that the tiny treasures on these pages were put there for you. You will find sweet, full circles of shared experiences as mothers and perhaps a few simple wonders that your heart will clutch closely, prompting you to dream of realms beyond what you have yet seen.

My Mama Robin prayer for you as you read this little book is that your mothering heart will be bolstered with courage and clarity.

And most of all hope.

When doubts filled my mind,
your comfort gave me renewed hope
and cheer.

PSALM 94:19, NLT

"HOPE" IS THE THING WITH FEATHERS—
THAT PERCHES IN THE SOUL—
AND SINGS THE TUNE WITHOUT THE WORDS—
AND NEVER STOPS—AT ALL.

—Emily Dickinson
"'Hope' is the thing with feathers"

Being a mother
means that your heart is no longer yours;
it wanders wherever your children do.

—ATTRIBUTED TO GEORGE BERNARD SHAW

Part One

NOW:

Embracing the Newness of MomLife

My heart floated on a river of love for you
Until the day you arrived.
Your tiny fingers curled around mine,
And my whole being was swept into a sea of wonder.

—RJG

This Just Got Real

𝓛ook at you. You're a mother!

As prepared as you were for the grand arrival of your little one, nothing has been exactly as you thought it would be. And yet the moment you first kissed those pudgy cheeks, you felt it. A tremor and a thrill settled on you. This just got real.

You have been entrusted with a brand-new, tiny soul.

What do you do now?

May I share some simple thoughts that will help you navigate this new season?

Trust. Trust the instincts that God affixed to your DNA when He knit you together in your mother's womb.

Delight. Take delight in all the coos and wiggles. Marvel at the miracle for a long moment without allowing a single worry to cross your mind.

Dream. Dream of all the days ahead as you set sail with your wee one to an uncharted future on a sea of possibilities.

Hope. Above all, hold on to hope as you see yourself drifting further away from your former life and as the waves of emotions roll.

Hope will pour over you a fresh dose of courage every morning.

> *You are this child's mother. You are able. This is a blessing.*

Hope will calm your spirit in the middle of the night.

> *You have done all you can. Your little one is asleep. Now you rest as well.*

Hope will compel you to give all you have and then give a little more.

> *You can do this. You have resources inside that you haven't even tapped yet.*

Take heart. Hold on to hope. The winds will blow. The storms will rage. But most days the sun will shine, and you will come to understand true love as you put your hope in God.

We have this hope as an anchor for the soul.

HEBREWS 6:19, NIV

A Mother's Prayer for Sleep

Father God,

Cover me with the gift of sleep. Deep, sweet sleep. I am so tired. I need to recharge.

In a few hours my baby will cry for me, and I will respond with all I have to give. Replenish my body and my spirit now, I ask. Give me what I need so that I can give my little one what she needs.

Cover me with the gift of peace. Deep, sweet peace. I want to—I need to—close my eyes and believe that all is well and will be well. You watch over me as I sleep. You watch over my little one as she sleeps.

Let us both sleep in heavenly peace.

Cuddles and Coos

PINK FLESH PRESSED AGAINST MY CHEEK,
TINY FINGERS CURLED UP TIGHT,
GENTLE COOS OF SUCH DELIGHT—
IT IS NO SECRET:
YOU'VE CAPTURED MY HEART.

—RJG

He gives children to the woman who has none and makes her a happy mother.

PSALM 113:9, NCV

Daily Exercise

$\mathcal{W}$e all know that finding exercise recommendations for new mothers is pretty easy. With a few clicks of a mouse, you can watch videos that demonstrate movements to strengthen your core, fortify your back muscles, and help all the other slightly wobbly places to regain their dignity.

May I add one more exercise recommendation to your options?

This one is the most essential because it is for your spirit.

Do this daily, or as often as needed, and it will strengthen the deepest part of you. The part that will last forever.

Say to yourself,

SHAME OFF
GRACE ON

Try it again, and this time, fill in your name at the end. Our Father knows you by name, and this exercise in faith is the message He has repeated to His children throughout the ages.

Go ahead.

Say it like you mean it. Come on! Say it aloud!

SHAME OFF YOU, _____.
GRACE ON YOU, _____.

Pretty great, huh? Want to do it again? Go ahead. Feel the burn. The shame is gone. The grace is on.

This ancient and powerful internal exercise was devised especially for you by the Lover of your soul. He removed your shame when He took on all your guilt. He extends to you grace upon grace upon grace.

Endless grace.

Do this soul-strengthening exercise continually, and you will find that you can mother your children longer, faster, better, and with more unencumbered joy than you thought your weary soul could muster.

Guaranteed.

Exercise daily in God—no spiritual flabbiness, please!
Workouts in the gymnasium are useful,
but a disciplined life in God is far more so,
making you fit both today and forever.
You can count on this.
Take it to heart.

1 TIMOTHY 4:8-9, MSG

Mercy in the Morning, Grace in the Evening

My daddy was the son of a Kentucky coal miner. When he was in a jovial mood, you could hear him singing around the house,

SUGAR IN THE MORNING, SUGAR IN THE EVENING, SUGAR AT SUPPA' TIME.

I smile now when I think of it because I can't imagine any mama in this generation singing to her children about sugar.

Now it's more like

PESTICIDE-FREE BANANAS IN THE MORNING, HOMEGROWN SQUASH IN THE EVENING, ORGANIC, FREE-RANGE, GLUTEN-FREE, NON-GMO, FAIR-TRADE CHICKEN AT SUPPERTIME.

I was thinking of my dad the other day and how he surrendered his life to Christ when I was in second grade. His commitment was solidified at a family weekend retreat at Forest Home

Conference Center in California. Billy Graham was the speaker, but what I remember most was that the three of us kids had the thrill of sleeping in bunk beds in a real mountain cabin.

My dad's relationship with Jesus encompassed our family and led us to a solid church where eventually my siblings and I all had our weddings. The spiritual foundation established for us in that community was one of mercy and grace.

Perhaps you are a new mother who didn't come from a family with two parents. You didn't have a childhood that included solid spiritual direction. The challenge to give your child what you never had is daunting. You are aware of the gaps in your own understanding of biblical principles, and ever with you is the desire to "do it right."

Here's the good news: There's hope!

There is a simple starting place for all mothers, no matter when your spiritual birth took place. What matters is that you've come to Christ. You've surrendered your life and all that is in it to the Savior who gave His life for you. He demolished all your offenses against the One True, Holy God. He invites you to live in the freedom He gives you.

Now believe.

Believe what God said when He declared that His "mercies . . . are new every morning" (Lamentations 3:22-23).

The moment you open your eyes each new day, God's tender mercies are being poured out on you. Decide afresh that you will put aside all past failures. Don't start the day reciting a long list of everything that has gone awry. Instead, believe that He is with you and in you and for you, and in all things He is accomplishing His purposes for you.

As the day unfolds and the circus of your life begins, believe that what matters to your Heavenly Father is that you live a blameless life.

Not perfect.

Blameless.

There is a huge difference between the two. *Perfect* means you try and try and strive some more to get everything right without any hint of failure. And yet, being human, eventually you'll fail at something.

You will never be perfect.

But you can be blameless.

Here's how:

Every day, dive into the adventure of motherhood with abandon. Be teachable. Give it all you've got. When you slip up, admit it. Be honest with God, with yourself, with others. See the moment, the actions, the words, and the heart attitude for what they were.

You were wrong.

Plain and simple.

That's why we all need a Savior. None of us is perfect.

But we can be blameless when we admit our failure, ask for forgiveness, and then believe—I mean really believe—that we have been released from the guilt and all the shame.

Switch your mothering standard from perfect to blameless, and you will be free.

When you come to the end of the day, don't take a list of failures to bed with you. They were all forgiven, remember? You dealt with them the moment you realized you messed up.

Now you are blameless. The accuser can't hold a single infraction against you.

Not perfect. Not faultless.

Blameless.

Be sure you don't switch out your list of daily blunders for a list of your husband's failures, or your children's, or your mother's, or your friend's, or your dog's. It will get too crowded in that bed of yours if you take all their foibles with you under those covers. Instead, forgive. Extend grace.

Extravagant grace.

Grace for yourself first of all because that's what God has given to you. If He says you're forgiven, who are you to tell Him He's wrong? Cozy yourself under the comforter of His grace and sleep the peaceful sleep of a mother who knows that when she rises the next day, God's mercies will be fresh and new all over again.

I can almost imagine that this is the song our Heavenly Papa sings over you:

MERCY IN THE MORNING, GRACE IN THE EVENING, BLAMELESS AT SUPPERTIME.

And to that blessing, perhaps He would add,

BE MY GRACE-FILLED MAMA, AND LOVE ME ALL THE TIME.

Are you tired?
Worn out?
Burned out on religion?
Come to me.
Get away with me and you'll recover your life.
I'll show you how to take a real rest.
Walk with me and work with me—watch how I do it.
Learn the unforced rhythms of grace.
I won't lay anything heavy or ill-fitting on you.
Keep company with me
and you'll learn to live freely and lightly.

MATTHEW 11:28-30, MSG

Daughter of Mine

Just yesterday you were an infant, safely nestled in my arms;

today you are a mother.

You hold your son with the wide-eyed look of a newly initiated member of this

ancient, maternal fellowship.

With deep affection I welcome you.

I see your courage. I smile at your tenderness.

Amidst all the celebration, part of me aches silently because I remember

so clearly

this coronation into motherhood.

I remember how badly I wanted to get it right—how I wanted to always do my best and

give it my all. I didn't want to make a single mistake.

But I did.

And so will you. And it's okay.

Now listen.

Listen with your heart.

Here is the truth that must be spoken, O daughter of mine:

YOU ARE ENOUGH.

YOU ARE ENOUGH woman, mother, chef, nester, teacher, friend, housekeeper, entertainer, lullaby singer, storyteller, and puppeteer.

YOU ARE ENOUGH, and you have enough of all that is needed for today

—just today—

as you nurture this tiny human soul delivered into your care.

Don't be afraid.

Don't worry about what lies ahead. Embrace the adventure with your whole heart.

Day by day

the Lord will make you equal to the task.

All you have to do is what is set before you today.

Just today.

Motherhood is on-the-job training.

There is no rehearsal. No do-over days. Just today.

And just you.

You are the one God chose to be the mother of this little one.

And YOU ARE ENOUGH.

Rest in the peace that comes with this timeless truth,

O Daughter of Mine.

—RJG

For this child I prayed.

~ 1 SAMUEL 1:27

Falling in Love

You must be falling in love.

Toddler love.

I keep hearing you say the same phrases to your son that you once said to the man you married.

For instance,

when your son picked the lock on the childproof gate and took off down the stairs, you said,

"I can't take my eyes off of you."

When he was about to let go and dash into the street, you said,

"I love it when you hold my hand."

When he was supposed to be napping,
but you heard a loud thump from his room, your lips uttered,

"This boy makes my heart pound wildly."

When his cute face was covered in yogurt and bananas, and he wanted to kiss you,
I heard you say,

"You have the sweetest kisses."

When he came down with the stomach flu in the middle of the night,
you texted me the same words you used on the eve of your engagement:

"In my wildest dreams, I never imagined it could be like this."

–RJG

Love Lessons

Young heart, so brave,
so tender and true,
you came to us fresh from heaven
that we might learn the art
of selfless love
by spending our lives
with you.

—RJG

More Than

I was wrong.
My darling daughter, I was wrong.

I told you that you were enough.
Enough woman, mother, chef, teacher, puppeteer . . .

Today I saw the deeper truth as I watched
you accomplish heroic acts of everyday motherhood.
Now I know that you are not enough.
No.

The truth is . . .
YOU ARE MORE THAN.

MORE THAN
the length of your days
or the breadth of your knowledge.

MORE THAN
yesterday's accomplishments
or tomorrow's goals.

YOU ARE MORE THAN you were when you started this
journey into motherhood.

MORE THAN
a diaper-changing station
or a twenty-four-hour concession stand.

YOU ARE MORE THAN you can see;
more than your thin emotions can feel.

YOU ARE MORE THAN the sum of all your parts.
MORE THAN what you saw in the mirror this morning.
MORE THAN what you told yourself three
minutes ago.

22

Listen. Hear this and treasure it in your heart.

You don't have to
do more
be more
give more
try more.

YOU ARE ALREADY MORE.
MORE THAN *you know.*

You are
a song in the night
a gentle touch
a calm word
an assuring smile
a soft kiss.

You are not just enough, dear little mama.
YOU ARE MORE THAN.

In all things, for all days,
YOU ARE MORE THAN *a conqueror through*
Him who
handcrafted you
unfailingly loves you
continually guides you.

He is the One who placed on you the care of
these eternal souls—
the Giver of all good gifts.

The One who is
and was
and is to come.

He will give you more than enough to see you
through.

—RJG

In all these things we are more than conquerors through him who loved us.

ROMANS 8:37

Don't miss the miracles in front of you
by gazing too longingly
at the moments
behind you.

—RJG

25

Before-and-After Selfies

Yes, sweetheart,
I know.
Your hair is frightful.

And yes,
I know.
You never used to go out
in public without makeup.

Those images were your
before selfies.

This is you now.
The young mother you.
And you are beautiful.

You are.

The image you now
bear in your
after selfie
tells of
beauty drawn from a deeper well.

Your eyes reflect wisdom born of wider knowledge.
Knowledge of the inner strength
you didn't know you had until
that first contraction
came upon you.

Your body gave all it could give
when you ushered that tiny human into this world.

Your appearance now reflects all that is
selfless and true.
You radiate
the universal beauty of motherhood.

Of course you feel shell-shocked.
Of course your little one just ruined
what used to be
your favorite shirt.

Soon enough
the hair, the makeup, the clothes—
all those familiar additions
to your beauty—
will return to your life.

For now, let me gaze upon
the exquisite beauty
of you—
the truest,
most womanly expression
of you.

You wear so effortlessly
the only accessory you need right now—
a well-fed, much-loved, fragile bundle of new life,
swaddled and serene,
cradled in your arms.

—RJG

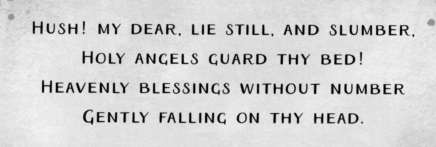

HUSH! MY DEAR, LIE STILL, AND SLUMBER,
HOLY ANGELS GUARD THY BED!
HEAVENLY BLESSINGS WITHOUT NUMBER
GENTLY FALLING ON THY HEAD.

-Isaac Watts
"A Cradle Hymn"

At day's end I'm ready for sound sleep,
for you, GOD, have put my life back together.

—— PSALM 4:8, MSG

A mother's arms
are made of tenderness,
and children sleep
soundly in them.

—VICTOR HUGO

Les Misérables

A True Mom

You tried, you waited, you hoped, you prayed.
Today they arrived—
the children born in your heart long ago.
Not one baby,
but three children . . .
arriving on your doorstep,
with suitcases.
Beautiful, timid, and a little bit wild.
You chose them,
and God chose you.

Today a family was born.
The adventures begin as you learn to live
With every mother's discomfort
of seeing the worst in you burst forth
while quickly chased
by the best in you.

Your heart will forever feel
slightly desperate
and slightly awestruck
at the same time.

The years will roll out in curves
and bumps and twists and ruts,
and you will do what you practiced
so well
before your children arrived.
You will try, you will wait, you will hope, and you will pray.
These are the time-honored dance steps of every mother.

You are a true mom.
Welcome to the ballroom.

—RJG

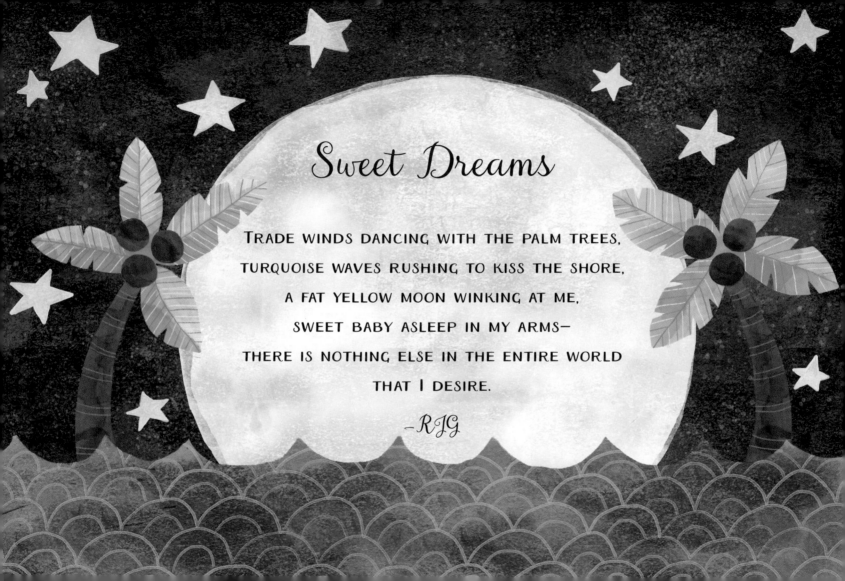

Sweet Dreams

TRADE WINDS DANCING WITH THE PALM TREES,
TURQUOISE WAVES RUSHING TO KISS THE SHORE,
A FAT YELLOW MOON WINKING AT ME,
SWEET BABY ASLEEP IN MY ARMS—
THERE IS NOTHING ELSE IN THE ENTIRE WORLD
THAT I DESIRE.

-RJG

First-Month Prayer

Lord, speak to me
In the cavern of my heart
Where darkness has hemmed me in.
I'm so, so tired.

Speak to me
In the corners of my thoughts
Where I have become a hoarder of fears.
Is he breathing? Is he breathing? Is he breathing?

Speak to me
In the cacophony of
Infant cries and dryer buzzes and microwave beeps.
I don't even know what day it is.

Speak to me, Father.
Tell me it's going to be all right.
Tell me I'm going to make it.
I'm not alone. You're with me. Always with me.
Always with us. ♥

-RJG

Your Beautiful Chaos

Somehow you've come to believe that you must make your life look lovely in this mothering season, a Pinterest image that dozens—no, hundreds—will like and pin. You think you need to do something more to make it so.

You do not.

You only need to do what you do each day with a selfless spirit, a tender heart, and all the gusto your giddy soul can muster.

It doesn't matter how messy and fragmented your life appears to be right now.

All that matters is that you love well.

Love the sweetness in his little smile when you lift him from the crib each morning.

Love the way her tiny toes wiggle when you change her diaper.

Love the way they fall asleep in their car seats on the way home with snacks in their hair and books splayed open across their bellies.

Love this beautiful chaos that your life has become.

Most of all, love yourself for being brave and content and teachable in all the unlovely moments.

A deep sacredness is growing in your life.

Let it grow.

You are becoming the next-season version of you.

And that is the loveliest and most sacred everyday wonder there is.

They brought little children to Him, that He might touch them; but the disciples rebuked those who brought them. But when Jesus saw it, He was greatly displeased and said to them, "Let the little children come to Me, and do not forbid them; for of such is the kingdom of God. Assuredly, I say to you, whoever does not receive the kingdom of God as a little child will by no means enter it." And He took them up in His arms, laid His hands on them, and blessed them.

MARK 10:13-16, NKJV

Mama Art

$\mathcal{E}$very mother is an artist.

She is a cocreator.

A receiver and a giver of life.

On drab days when all the colors on your mother-hood palette seem gray and your imagination seems to have evaporated, remember this:

You are infused with the resurrection power of the Master Craftsman, who knit together your molecules with such ingenuity that there is no one else in all the universe exactly like you—nor will there ever be.

You are empowered with the vast resourcefulness of

37

the One who scooped out the oceans with His hands and formed the delicate wings of the hummingbird with those same fingers. He spoke, and all the stars took their places in the heavens, ready for their celestial dance, playing to a full house every night for thousands of years.

You are rich in possibilities.

The Great Gardener has planted rows and rows of tiny inspirations in your heart. When you feel the nudge to try a new recipe, capture a sacred moment in a photo, or make up a silly song with your little one, it is because His Spirit is alive in you, stirring up your ingenuity and encouraging you to harvest the abundance of inspirations He planted there.

You are His workmanship—His poem—His creative expression. In your lifetime, in your singular way, with your gifting, you are perfectly positioned and abundantly equipped to express life in an art form that is distinct to you.

What is your form of Mama Art? Do you create . . .

- *art on a plate with vegetables from your own garden?*
- *a haven with paint and furniture, window coverings, and pillows?*
- *words, music, and stories under indoor tents on rainy days?*
- *clothing and beanies, cuddly quilts and bows?*

- *love notes in lunch boxes or colorful charts on the kitchen wall?*
- *with silence, the gift of listening, the tenderness of a soothing touch?*
- *laughter, silly songs, and funny faces that make the tears go away?*

Only you, unique you, can create the beautiful art you do in the way that you do.

Don't hold back—go be a cocreator today.

Explore the endless possibilities of your Mama Art.

Express the beauty fully with love, confidence,

and sweet abandon.

She opens her mouth with wisdom,
and the teaching of kindness is on her tongue.
She looks well to the ways of her household
and does not eat the bread of idleness.

PROVERBS 31:26-27

You know you're a mom
when you say at least once a day,
"I'm not cut out for this job,"
but you know
you wouldn't trade it for anything.

—Author Unknown

If you want a happy family,
if you want a holy family,
give your hearts to love.

—Mother Teresa

Make a careful exploration of who you are
and the work you have been given,
and then sink yourself into that.
Don't be impressed with yourself.
Don't compare yourself with others.
Each of you must take responsibility
for doing the creative best you can
with your own life.

GALATIANS 6:4-5, MSG

New Dreams

Tonight as you watched the sunset,
I saw you look over your shoulder.

Were you thinking of what might have been
but never was?

I saw the tears you blinked away.
I recognized the brave upward curve of your lips.

My darling, please—
go ahead.
Don't hold back.
Find a sheltered haven
and intentionally
grieve the loss.

Speak to the vaporous doubts,
those harassing ghosts.
Tell them they are your companions no more.

Then wash your face
and come back to us.

Embrace the life you have.
Put your hope in God.

Tonight
you will finally fall asleep
dreaming
of all that is yet to come.

—RJG

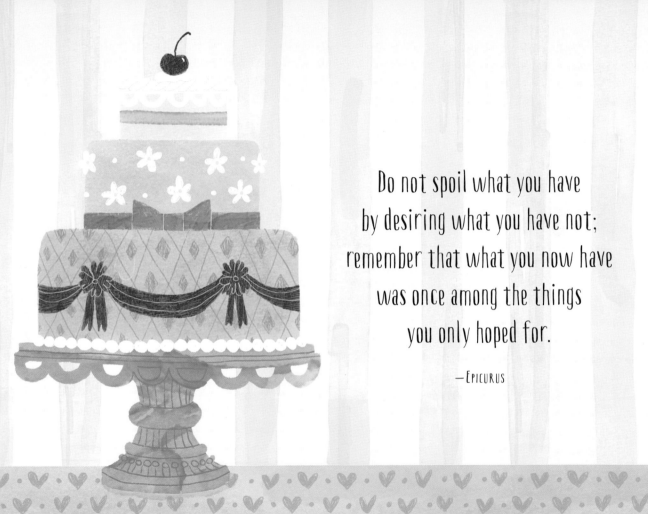

Do not spoil what you have
by desiring what you have not;
remember that what you now have
was once among the things
you only hoped for.

—Epicurus

Her World

She looks up at you
with fearless awe. You are her world.
From your body
she draws her nourishment.
From your eyes
she drinks deep peace.
From the sound of your voice
she receives comfort.

She touches your face
with curiosity.
You are her world.

With her fingertips
she discovers tenderness.
From your kisses on her pudgy palm
she senses sweetness.
Within the landscape of your features
she memorizes the way home.

You are her world.

—RJG

It is not a slight thing
when they,
who are so fresh from God,
love us.

—CHARLES DICKENS

The Old Curiosity Shop

When Day Is Done

Streamers of pink satin ribbons flutter across the primrose sky.

The sun, looking like a great orange-and-yellow-frosted sugar cookie, is about to be dunked into the ocean's wide-rimmed cup.

The day is done.

And here we sit, nested in pockets of tawny sand; pockets that still hold the warmth of the fleeting day. The ever-dancing breezes make their farewells, brushing kisses across our cheeks as off they go. Somewhere across the sapphire sea they will greet a new day as it opens its eyes.

But here, the day is done.

A match is lit, and the gathered kindling sparks. Slowly the flames rise like slender arms, eager to embrace the driftwood. A settled hush comes over the beach as twilight draws close this circle of friends.

My young daughter Rachel sits perfectly still, her back straight, gazing into the dancing flames. She's careful not to move as my friend Claire folds Rachel's hair into one long braid.

In the south corner of the sky, a full moon rises. A perfectly round sugar cookie, unfrosted. Fresh from heaven's oven.

Claire's little Anna cuddles up next to me. I take the sleepy toddler into my lap, where she settles in with a contented sigh. The scent of the sun's caresses from the day rises from Anna's golden hair, filling me with memories of when my own children were this small. On her feet she wears booties made of caramel-colored sand knit in place, grain by grain, with dried salt water. Her lips pucker into the shape of a tender heart as she falls asleep in my arms. In the gentle rhythm of Anna's unlabored breaths there is no fear. No worry. No anxiety over tomorrow's troubles.

The day is done.

I lift my chin to the heavens. The vast canopy of the cosmos is alive with stars and spinning planets too numerous to count. The One who put them into motion is the One who now holds me in His everlasting arms. He bids me to now rest in Him with the peace of a child. His child.

The day is done.

You are not a wild wind, sent to chase the sun into the blazing tomorrow.

Rest.

As Anna slumbers in my arms, my heart catches a ride on the slow-rising alabaster moon. All my cares are tossed aside—tinder for the campfire. I leave them there and dream of tomorrow with all the simple hopes of a much-loved child.

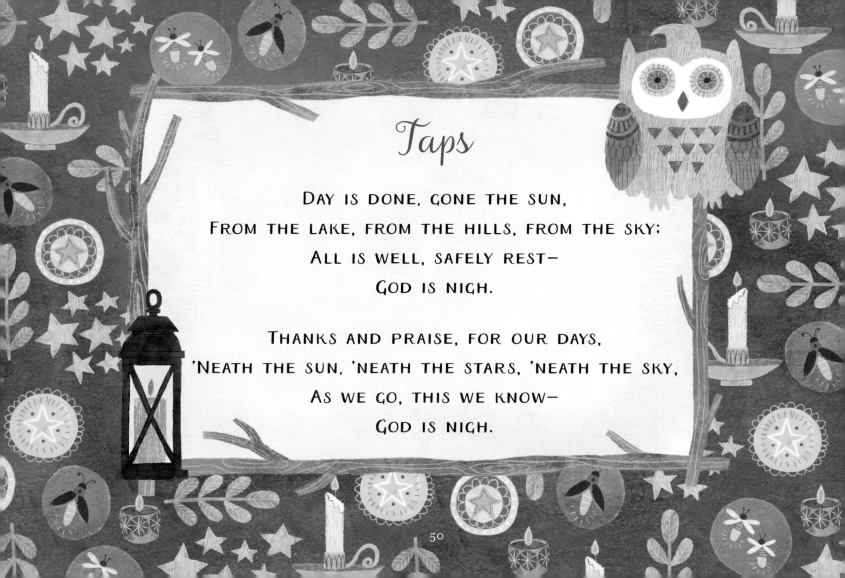

Taps

Day is done, gone the sun,
From the lake, from the hills, from the sky;
All is well, safely rest—
God is nigh.

Thanks and praise, for our days,
'Neath the sun, 'neath the stars, 'neath the sky,
As we go, this we know—
God is nigh.

Yes, dear friends,
we are already God's children, right now,
and we can't even imagine
what it is going to be like later on.
But we do know this,
that when he comes we will be like him,
as a result of seeing him as he really is.

1 JOHN 3:2, TLB

Mothering Alone

I know you feel abandoned, dear one.
Your mother left this earth before she even knew
that you were about to become a mother too.

If she were here she would say,
My darling girl, you're doing a great job,
you really are.

It's going to be okay.
Take heart.
Take hope.
Be courageous and love with all you've got.

You've already navigated many sharp turns
and taken on your new role with tenderness—
tenderness and love. Much, much love.

Your mother would be so proud of you.
She would adore your little one;
she would find great joy in this new-mother version of you.

It's going to be okay.
Take heart.
Take hope.
Be content and love with all you've got.

You carry with you the best of her
and merge it effortlessly
with the best of you.

Glimmers of her loveliness have blended
with shimmers of your beauty.
Together they stir within the heart of your precious child.

It's going to be okay.
Take heart.
Take hope.
Be at peace and love with all you've got.

—RJG

Even if my father and mother abandon me,
the LORD will hold me close.

PSALM 27:10, NLT

Aprons and Prayers

Susanna Wesley gave birth to nineteen children. Ten of them lived to adulthood.

She was born in England in 1669 and married Samuel, a twenty-six-year-old clergyman and poet, when she was nineteen.

What was motherhood like for a young woman such as Susanna in that period of history? It wasn't very similar to what motherhood looks like today. Or was it?

See if you can imagine some of her challenges.

Children: Susanna had two sets of twins. All four of them died when they were babies. She had five other babies who died in infancy. One of them was accidently smothered. Eight of her children were still alive when she died in London in 1742 at the age of seventy-three.

Marriage: Susanna's husband left her after a minor dispute. For more than a year Susanna raised their children on her own. Samuel returned, but the troubles continued when shots were fired at their home and their fields were set on fire by parishioners who opposed his political stance. Their house burned down twice.

Finances: Samuel ended up in debtor's prison twice, and as a result their children were bullied.

How's your life looking in comparison right about now?

A greater question is, How could a mother of so many children, facing such adversity, find a way to influence and inspire her children to love God?

Susanna's secret was prayer.

Her sanctuary was under her apron.

That's right. Her apron. In the middle of the daily bedlam, Susanna would pull her apron over her head and pray.

Whenever she entered her private apron tabernacle, her children knew that their names were on her lips. They also knew better than to disturb one of her spontaneous prayer meetings.

She once wrote, "I am content to fill a little space, if God be glorified."

Susanna may have filled a small space, but her children lived expansive lives. All three of Susanna's surviving sons became clergymen. John and Charles Wesley are known throughout the world as two of the greatest eighteenth-century evangelists and reformers. We still sing some of the more than six thousand hymns written by Charles.

Yes, I said six thousand hymns. John wrote many of the lyrics along with Charles. Two of my favorites are "Hark! The Herald Angels Sing" and "O for a Thousand Tongues to Sing."

God heard Susanna's prayers for her children.

He hears your prayers for your children.

Regardless of the many obstacles in your path, you can pray. You must pray. Every day. Fill your little space with prayer.

If your life, your children, your marriage, or your finances fall apart, you know what to do. Get into your fight-mode position. Ready?

Aprons up!

Let the prayers begin.

Mother
means selfless devotion,
limitless sacrifice,
and love
that passes understanding.

—Author Unknown

God . . .
rekindles burned-out lives with fresh hope.

1 SAMUEL 2:7-8, MSG

I remember
my mother's prayers
and they have always followed me.
They have clung to me all my life.

—Abraham Lincoln

How joyful are those who fear the LORD
and delight in obeying his commands.
Their children will be successful everywhere;
an entire generation of godly people will be blessed.

PSALM 112:1-2, NLT

Havens

I have a special little love seat tucked into the corner of our patio where I go each morning with my Bible, my journal, and a cuppa tea. When the doves are cooing and bobbing about on the grass, I open my laptop, and this sacred space becomes my writing hideaway. Tales unfold in my imagination, and I type in rhythm with the morning breezes that relentlessly rustle the palm trees.

Most afternoons, this place becomes the hallowed ground where my daughter comes with her eighteen-month-old son. She blows bubbles for him to chase, and when he wears himself out, I stretch out beside him on the rug and sing "Jesus Loves Me" in his ear as he fiddles with a fistful of circles, triangles, and squares, trying to fit them into their assigned places in the wooden box puzzle.

In this puzzled universe, this corner is my assigned place. This love seat with the azure-blue cushion under the soothing wind chimes. Here, with these people, doing these things. This is my haven.

This is where, on many evenings, my husband and I stand with our arms around each other and watch the sun melt into the western sky. In the afterglow we have often dined here, dreamed here, and named the geckos that race across the pale yellow stucco walls. This is where we watch the moon rise.

When we moved into this cottage five years ago, the cracked cement slab did not look like a sacred-space-in-waiting. The sliding screen doors had been shredded by neighborhood cats, and black mold was growing in the corner where the garden hose had been left to drip, drip, drip.

It became a sacred space when we set it apart.

We did that by cleaning it up, repairing what was torn, and christening this small patio with candlelit conversations, a few cushioned chairs, an end table, and a white orchid from Pukalani Nursery. These few feet of lanai became set apart as a destination, and I believe that's when this outdoor room transformed into a sacred space. It became the place in our home where words, songs, and prayers could mingle undistracted with the unseen but always felt presence of our great God.

I love our little redeemed corner of this enormous world.

What about you? Do you have a sacred space in your home?

I believe every woman, and especially every mother, needs a designated sacred space wherever she lives. Even if she's renting. Even if her place is tiny. Even if she won't live there for very long.

You need a place that's yours.

You don't need a lot. It could be as big as a corner chair where you cuddle your babies and close your eyes to listen and pray. The holiness happens when that designated space is set apart. You know it's your haven because when you narrow down all the options, it's the one place in your home where you feel the heartbeat of your life coming through the strongest. It has become your sacred space.

The bigger picture in all this is that sacred spaces in our homes are tangible reflections of the invisible sacred spaces that dwell hidden inside us.

We are just little souls. But we, too, have been set apart, you and I. We have been redeemed, cleaned up, and designated for a specific purpose.

Communion.

Connection.

Reflection.

Our lives have been turned into sacred spaces.

This is especially true for mothers. When our children are looking for comfort and the purest forms of communion, they narrow down all the people around them to just "Mama." Their hearts beat with the deepest peace when they echo the sounds of ours. You are your child's destination.

Think of it.

You have become a human destination where your little ones are drawn to come and just be. To chase dreams and solve puzzles. To listen. To rest. To feel the closeness of your love.

We are sacred spaces, you and I. Destinations graced with love and hope and peace.

We are havens.

In a world of noise, movement, and options, you, dearest little mama, are an ever-fixed destination for your children. You are now, and always will be, their haven.

A mother's heart holds many charms
And love is ever in her arms.
And in her eyes a faith divine,
And home is you,
Mother Mine.

—CARRIE JACOBS-BOND

from "Mother Mine"

The Golden Rule of Golden Moments

This week you plodded down the trail of motherhood with heavy feet. Each step seemed to weigh you down, lead you off course, rub another blister on your soul.

It was agony.

Nothing you tried turned out the way you intended: Not the playdate. Not the new kind of chicken nuggets. Not the jammies that arrived a week late and a size too small. Not the hoped-for extra-long nap so you could take a shower and actually shave your legs.

And definitely not the moment a toy ended up in the toilet and caused an overflow that ruined the new bathroom rug and turned you into a growling mama bear armed with enough disinfectant to clean a submarine.

Your life looks nothing like the radiant images every mother you know is posting on Instagram this week. You're certain that the problem is you. Only you. Your trek through motherhood is neither smooth nor enjoyable nor beautiful. It's a mess. You're a mess.

Why is it that every other woman in your circle who is walking this same trail manages to do it with panache? For instance, this one—with the twins. How is it that she can manage to make perfect little pink cupcakes for her well-behaved daughters, who are wearing bows in their hair and having a picnic with their dolls? And it isn't even their birthday.

You click on the video she posted of their golden afternoon. Look at her: Smiling. Twirling. Laughing. Her girls gaze at her adoringly. Those seventeen seconds of mothering bliss demolish you. Why? Because she's added a Scripture verse in her comments. She's happy, adored, talented, *and* spiritual. It's simply unnatural.

And look. Already 427 people "like" her post. They like her. They like her life. They like the way she elevates mothering to an art form and not a battleground trudge like the one you've been on all week.

You look away and scold yourself. What you feel is envy. You know it. How can you make it stop? Your finger hovers over the "unfriend" button. Her path of motherhood has been paved. All the rocks, mud, thorns, and stinging bees have been removed from her life. Of course she's twirling, grinning, and laughing at the time to come. You would be, too, if you had her life.

Then it happens.

You look up from your phone, and your world seems to have hit pause. Your little monkeys are not jumping on the bed. They are sitting side by side in the recliner, looking at a book. The waning sunlight is pouring through the window, skimming the tops of their heads, crowning them with halos.

You lift your phone and capture the golden moment. Joy wells up. Sweetness and hope flood your thoughts. You have to post this. Now.

Within seconds the winsome, rare, stunning image is live for all the world to see. You watch for affirmations. Like-like-like-like-like-like-like-comment.

"You have such adorable babies. I wish mine would cuddle up like that. My life is a train wreck right now."

You start tapping a reply: "Oh, trust me. It's not like this. Ever." But then you pause.

Apparently, sometimes, it is like this. You have golden moments too. Just like every other mother. This is one of them.

You put down your phone and stand there in real time, in real life, taking in the beauty of your rare golden moment. Your children's voices carry across the room with the cadence of a lullaby. Your heart melts.

You draw in a deep breath, filling your soul with grace. This is the day you choose to finally make peace with the golden rule of the golden moments of motherhood:

ANY MOTHER,
AT ANY TIME,
WHO CAN CAPTURE ANY ONE OF HER RARE
GOLDEN MOMENTS
AND POST IT FOR ALL THE WORLD TO SEE
SHOULD BE CELEBRATED
BUT
NEVER ENVIED.

Strength and dignity are her clothing, and she laughs at the time to come.

PROVERBS 31:25

What a Mother Thinks

I love you so much.

There is no way I can possibly put into words how proud I am of you.

You're absolutely beautiful.

Sometimes when our eyes meet,

it's like gazing into a reflecting pool.

I see in you glimmers of my past.

Do you see in me hints of your future?

You are everything I ever prayed for.

There's nothing about you I'd change.

I love you more than you will ever know,

more than you will ever ask.

There's nothing I wouldn't give for you,

nothing I wouldn't do for you.

You are my daughter,

and I will always love you with a love so immense,

so eternal . . .

I could never find a way to squeeze it into words.

—RJG

Thou art thy mother's glass,
and she in thee
Calls back the lovely April
of her prime.

–William Shakespeare

"Sonnet 3"

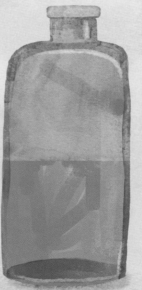

PART TWO

THEN:

Cherishing the Journey of MomLife

THE YEARS HAVE GATHERED UP ALL THE DAYS
AND TOSSED THEM INTO THE GALAXY OF MY THOUGHTS,
SETTING ABLAZE AN EVER-TWINKLING CONSTELLATION OF HOPE.

—RJG

A mother's hug
lasts long after she lets go.

— AUTHOR UNKNOWN

Waiting

Dear Baby, here beneath my heart,
I thought that you might come today;
the timing just seemed right.

But the stars are out,
and the moon is high,
and sheepishly I wonder why
I try to arrange the plans of God.

For now I know
you will not come
until the One who holds eternity
rustles your soft cocoon and
whispers in tones that I will not hear,
"It's time, precious gift. Now it's time."

—RJG

Every child born into the world
is a new incarnate thought of God,
an ever fresh and radiant possibility.

—Kate Douglas Wiggin

Mothering by Heart

I hold you in my arms, young prince. You sleep in sweet, heavenly peace. Yet I wonder if you'd be so calm if you knew the truth: I am your mother. And I don't have the slightest idea what I'm doing.

You are my first baby. My only son. I was just getting used to being pregnant, and now here you are! And you are so very, very real.

I've been preparing for your arrival for months. I've read the books. Well, some of them. A few pages. I've listened to my friends, who give me endless advice. They're all experienced, you know, because they have their own babies. But you're different. You're my baby. And they don't know a thing about you.

I do. I know all about the way you kick and wiggle. I've already memorized the way you smell, like a fresh-from-the-earth daffodil. I know about the way your lower lip quivers when you're about to cry. I know that your wispy hair is the most luxuriously soft thing that has ever touched my cheek.

Yet I admit there's much I don't know. In the hospital I had to be instructed on how to nurse you. Yesterday my mother showed me how to bathe you in the sink. I don't have a clue how to clear up diaper rash. I get queasy at the sight of blood. I don't sew. I'm not good at papier-mâché volcanoes. My math skills are atrocious. And you might as well know right up front that wiggly teeth give me the heebie-jeebies.

However, I am very good at baking cookies. I know how to make indoor tents on rainy days. And I have my father's wonderful sense of humor, so I know how to laugh and how to make you laugh.

I'll sing you sweet songs in the night. I'll pray for you every day. I'll let you keep any animal you catch, as long as you can feed it. I'll call all your imaginary friends by their first names. I'll put love notes in your lunch box, and I'll swim with you in the ocean, even when I'm old. Perhaps the best thing about being your mother is that I get to share these privileges with the most incredible man in the world—your father.

Any credentials I have were not earned over coffee with friends. They weren't found in a book or taught in a class.

I am convinced that these tender intuitions are gifted to every new mother in the quiet moments when her baby is cradled in her arms, as you are now safely sheltered in mine.

This is where our Heavenly Father will teach me how to mother you by heart.

I will wait on the LORD . . .
And I will hope in Him.
Here am I and the children whom
the LORD has given me!

ISAIAH 8:17-18, NKJV

Rachel Elizabeth

Little Lamb, Gift of God,
you came into this world so fast and furious!
One moment I was gasping for air.
The next I pried my eyes open and greeted
your lizard-like pose upon my chest.
Imagine!
You were just born and already you
held your head up,
blinking your eyes in the brightness.
I reached out my heavier-than-lead arms
to touch you,
and your still-wet, trembling hand
clasped my eager finger.
Then you curled up into a ten-pound ball
of wailing flesh.

Today, at eighteen months,
you still come at me hard and fast.
I close my eyes for one moment
and there you are—
on top of the table, out the front door.
I'm exhausted
from monitoring your independence.
Such strength. Such determination.

Then comes a night like tonight,
when you fight sleep,
holding up that stiff neck so assuredly

until at last, in my arms, you yield,
a twenty-pound ball of helpless flesh.

My snuggly little lamb,
I smile at the future,
for I know the Good Shepherd;
I hear His voice.
He makes you to lie down in flannel crib sheets.
He restores my soul.
Surely goodness and mercy will follow us all the days of our lives.

−RJG

There was never a child so lovely
but his mother was glad to get him to sleep.

—Ralph Waldo Emerson

The LORD is my shepherd; I shall not want. He makes me to lie down in green pastures. . . . He restores my soul.

PSALM 23:1-3, NKJV

The Wish beneath My Pillow

I was going through our son's closet in a flurry of spring cleaning when I discovered a small unmarked box on the top shelf. I placed it on the edge of the bed, but the box toppled over, spilling a pair of infant-sized blue tennis shoes, along with a gift card written in my brother's scrawl: "His first pair of Nikes."

I held one of the cute little shoes in the palm of my hand.

Did our son ever have feet this tiny?

Inside the closet was a pair of high-top shoes he now wore regularly. I reached for one of them and held it in my other hand, comparing it to the baby shoe.

From this to this in only four years? How is that possible?

That night I watched my son's steps as he trotted to the dinner table. My eyes followed the heels of his bare feet as he climbed the stairs for bath time. He kicked in the tub, and the splashes went everywhere, like a whale's spout.

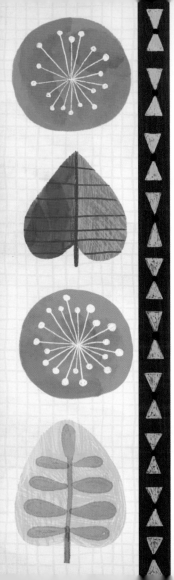

When I tucked him into bed, I grabbed his right foot and gave it a playful wrangle. His fleshy extremity no longer fit in the palm of my hand. There was nothing small or babyish or infant about this firstborn son of ours who had grown up while I was growing into my role as a mother.

I kissed him good-night. He quickly wiped the impression of my loving gesture off his cheek. I turned out the light and closed his door.

Where did my cuddly baby go?

I thought of how my mother's generation had a tradition of bronzing their babies' shoes and placing them on a shelf or prominently on the fireplace mantel. Those mini memorials seemed to be a way of freezing time. Of remembering when . . . and perhaps hoping yet . . . that another tiny pair of feet might soon visit that home.

When I crawled into bed that night, I took the baby-sized blue running shoe with me. I pressed the silly little thing against my cheek, gave it a kiss, and tucked it under my pillow.

Closing my eyes, I made a wish. It was the timeless wish of every mother who dared to hope for another pair of tiny feet with ten wiggly toes that would fill a pair of vacated baby shoes.

Children are a gift from God.

— PSALM 127:3, TLB

Wind Chasers

Today the wind invited the children and me to go outside and chase it.

So we did.

The trees, like dancing gypsies with golden coins in their hair, laughed above us as we frolicked down the street. The pockets of my jacket began to fill with autumn treasures, placed there by two sets of small hands.

Returning to the warm house, red-faced and breathless, the children asked me to unload their goodies onto the kitchen table. They were tickled with the joy of discovery. Along with twigs, feathers, leaves, and a few small rocks, my son had bagged a snail's shell—minus a snail.

My daughter laid out each of her big, amber-colored leaves before selecting the largest one to carefully use as a fan.

I watched as they arranged and rearranged each acorn, rock, leaf, and twig, preparing a centerpiece for the table. My daughter ran her fingers up the sides of a small tattered feather. When she turned it toward the window, the afternoon sunlight changed the feather's color from dull gray to bright silvery blue as she twirled it between her fingers.

My awestruck children spoke in hushed tones, lost in wonder, mesmerized by a handful of God's ordinary miracles.

With fumbling words I tried to express to my children how dearly treasured they were by God. They were and are His everyday wonders. His ordinary miracles. I wanted them to feel, in that moment, the pleasure of the Father and understand how He delights in collecting the ordinary of this world and bringing it into the warmth of His Kingdom. How His touch can turn the tattered into the dazzling.

Most of all, I wanted my children to know that their young hearts were not trinkets to be played with but were rare, priceless jewels in the hands of the King.

They looked at me with innocent eyes, blinking.

I knew then that I'd said enough. Such eternal truths can't be taught all at once by an intense and teary mother on a windy afternoon. It takes an entire childhood of days filled with ordinary miracles.

All your children shall be taught by the LORD,
And great shall be the peace of your children.

ISAIAH 54:13, NKJV

Giggles

THANK YOU,
MY LITTLE ONES,
FOR BRINGING WITH YOU
TENDER HEARTS AND
INNOCENT EYES.
I LOVE THE WAY
YOU SPRINKLE YOUR
CONTAGIOUS GIGGLES
ALL OVER MY LIFE.

-RJG

Autumn Dance

She stood a short distance from her guardian at the park this afternoon, her distinctive features giving away that, although her body had blossomed into young adulthood, her mind would always remain a child's.

My children ran and jumped and sifted sand through perfect, coordinated fingers. Caught up in fighting over a shovel, they didn't notice when the wind changed.

But she did.

A wild autumn wind spinning the leaves into amber flurries.

I called to my boisterous son and jostled my daughter. Time to go. Mom still has lots to do today.

My rosy-cheeked boy stood still, watching with wide-eyed fascination the gyrating dance of the Down syndrome girl as she scooped up leaves and showered herself with a twirling rain of autumn

jubilation. With each twist and hop she sang deep, earthy grunts—a canticle of praise meant only for the One whose breath causes the leaves to tremble from the trees.

"Hurry up. Let's go. Seat belts on?"

I started the car. In the rearview mirror, I studied the dancing girl one more time through misty eyes.

And then the tears came. Not tears of pity for her.

The tears were for me.

For I am too busy to frolic in the autumn leaves and far too sophisticated to publicly shout praises to my Creator. I am whole and intelligent and normal, and so I wept because I will never know the severe mercy that frees such a child and bids her, "Come. Dance in the autumn leaves."

You have taught the little children to praise you perfectly.

PSALM 8:2, TLB

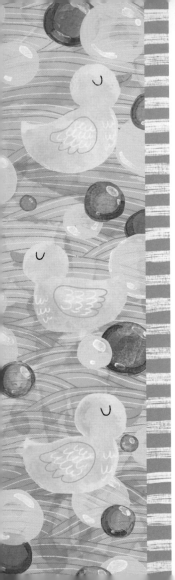

My Five-Year-Old Warrior

I watch my five-year-old lower himself into the steaming tub, where Mr. Bubble ministers to the wounds my son has suffered in battle today.

His arms bear scratches from the apple tree he scaled, and both knees are streaked with bloody reminders of his encounter with the sidewalk while charging on his trusty bike. Gently I towel down his bruised thighs, dotted with bites from relentless mosquitoes.

With vigor I rough up his sun-bleached hair and shoo him into his room, where he dresses for bed.

A story, a prayer, a hug, and a kiss.

My brave warrior closes his eyes, and I stand back, marveling that this long, sturdy body, lying lumpy beneath the covers, once fit in my arms and nursed at my breast. Many summer nights, just like this one, I rocked him. For hours I rocked and sang and prayed. Oh, how I prayed!

I close his door softly. My soldier needs his sleep.

Tomorrow great battles will be fought . . . in the sandbox, on his skateboard, with the neighborhood kids. He will return to me, bloodied and bruised, and there will be so little I can do. I have no power over scraped knees and stubbed toes.

But the real battle—the struggle against the temptation to stray from Jesus' way—has already begun in his young life.

And in that battle, I am the warrior.

I pray.

Oh, how I pray!

. . . that God will have the ultimate victory.

Be strong in the Lord and in his mighty power.
Put on all of God's armor so that you will be able
to stand firm against all strategies of the devil.

For we are not fighting against flesh-and-blood
enemies, but against evil rulers and authorities of
the unseen world, against mighty powers in this dark
world, and against evil spirits in the heavenly places.

EPHESIANS 6:10-12, NLT

The Wildflowers Are Gone

The Queen Anne's lace has all disappeared. So have the blue cornflowers and the dainty yellow buttercups. All summer long, the carefree wildflowers covered the knoll like a brightly embroidered shawl. Now they're gone. Dried and blown on the wind.

The hill has exchanged the laughing colors of summer for the rich, golden mantle of fall. Thoughtful shades of amber now stretch across the countryside. The season of brisk mornings, fat pumpkins, and translucent yellow maple leaves is upon us.

This morning the jolly yellow school bus rolled down our street and opened its squeaky door. My youngest stepped inside and was swallowed in one bite. I stood tall and brave, smiling and waving as she joined the other scrubbed faces staring out the windows.

Two other mothers asked if I'd like to join them for coffee. They were ready to celebrate. The start of the new school year! At last! Freedom!

I declined. "Maybe another morning," I said.

I strolled back to the house alone. My accordion heart was playing a different tune this year. A song of wildflowers gone. Blown on the wind. Another child off to school. Another summer spent.

I counted the summers I had left, like coins in a pocket. Summers when my son's hair would smell like chlorine from the pool as I kissed him good-night. Summers when my daughter would squeal at the sound of the ice cream truck coming down our street.

Inside my kitchen, the whistle of the teakettle cheered me. A steaming cup of comfort by the front window soothed the quiet ache. I closed my eyes and let the song of wildflowers gone roll over me.

For everything there is a season, and a time for every matter under heaven:

a time to be born, and a time to die;
a time to plant, and a time to pluck up what is planted;
a time to kill, and a time to heal;
a time to break down, and a time to build up;
a time to weep, and a time to laugh;
a time to mourn, and a time to dance;
a time to cast away stones, and a time to gather stones together;
a time to embrace, and a time to refrain from embracing;
a time to seek, and a time to lose;
a time to keep, and a time to cast away;
a time to tear, and a time to sew;
a time to keep silence, and a time to speak;
a time to love, and a time to hate;
a time for war, and a time for peace.

ECCLESIASTES 3:1-8

Deep, Cleansing Breaths

My friend Donna and I went shopping with our daughters. Her Natalie is sixteen; my Rachel is eight. The excursion, aimed at finding a bathing suit for Natalie, went something like this:

Natalie pulls a few bathing suits off the rack, and we head for the dressing room area. Donna begins taking deep, cleansing breaths, which strangely resemble the breathing techniques we were taught in our childbirth classes years ago. Rachel reaches for a few more swimsuits for Natalie to try on, and the two young ladies disappear behind the thick blue curtain.

A few moments later Rachel asks if we want to see. Of course we do. Back goes the curtain, and there stands Natalie in a bathing suit that slides over her every curve. Donna holds her breath until Natalie says she doesn't like it. I hear Donna letting out a "hee, hee, hee, whew."

Natalie returns to the dressing room. I watch the clock. It's about three minutes between changes. Rachel pulls back the curtain and displays suit number two on her life-size Barbie model. This one is a two-piece. Donna's breathing has turned noticeably more rapid.

Two minutes now between changes. We see suit number three, a rather low-cut black number. Donna sucks air in through clenched teeth. She seems a tad irritable, as if this transition is harder on her than it is on Natalie.

Here comes suit number four. Donna's face is red. She's clutching the sides of the chair and doesn't appear to be breathing at all. The curtain closes, and a stream of controlled breath passes through Donna's cracked lips. I consider going for ice chips, but it won't be long now, and I don't want to miss the Grand Conclusion. I coach Donna, telling her to hang in there. Just one more.

Rachel whips back the curtain, and Natalie turns around in number five, a lovely yet modest one-piece.

Donna's whole body pushes up from the chair, and with all her strength she announces, "That's the one!" Everyone is pleased. We all congratulate each other. I pass around a tin of breath mints.

Thus I came to know and understand the real reason they teach us Lamaze. It has nothing to do with the infant in the delivery room. It's all about the teenage daughter in the dressing room.

What a Mother Says

Oh, let me hold her!

Hush, little one.

Aren't you sleepy yet?

It's okay. Don't cry.

No, no. Don't touch.

Come to Mommy.

Take that out of your mouth. Yucky!

Tell Mommy if you need to go potty, okay?

Don't get into your brother's things.

Get back in bed—I just brought you a drink of water.

Pick up your toys.

Can you draw a picture for Grandma?

Hold still.

Go wash your hands.

Can you remember to bring it home tomorrow?

Did you practice?

I'm sure she still wants to be your friend.

Try looking under your bed.

You're not old enough yet.

Stop teasing your brother.

Where was it when you last saw it?

Go clean your room.

Come set the table.

Don't bite your nails.

Did you do your homework?

Get off the phone.

Eat your vegetables.

Did you tell me it was this Saturday?

Tell her you'll call her back.

You may not wear that to school.

There's a boy on the phone for you.

No, I need the car this afternoon.

Are you coming home this weekend? Next weekend?

When do we get to meet him?

Your ring is gorgeous!

How many are on the guest list?

The photographer is here.

You look stunning.

Yes, it was beautiful. All of it. And so were you.

Call us when you two get back.

We love you, too.

Good-bye, sweetheart.

–*RJG*

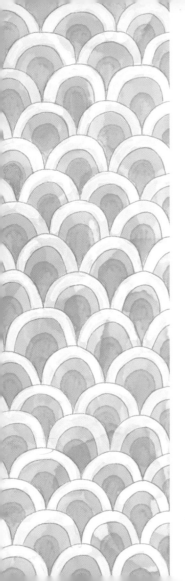

Holding Back Time

The kids and I went up to the lake today, eager to escape the heat. We settled in the sand at Kings Beach at Lake Tahoe, and off my children ran to play in the water.

I heard some girls giggling and scanned the shoreline until I saw the three bikini-clad middle-school girls splashing water at a boy and running before he could splash them back. Of course they returned for more splashes and more carefree giggling.

Ah, youth!

Under the August sun I wiggled my toes into the sand and thought back on my wonder years when my sister and I spent our summers innocently flirting with the boys at the beach. We were just like those girls, all arms and legs, chasing boys. Teasing them. Diligently planning our attacks until we got one of them to respond.

I smiled at those adorably skinny girls, feeling a sense of sisterhood. Of camaraderie. I marveled at the timeless elixir of sand, sun, and shore. Of how it is mixed vigorously by the summer wind and poured out on innocents, whisking them from childhood to adulthood. I watched as the skipping, giggling girls honed in on their unsuspecting victim and . . .

Suddenly I sprang from my chair.

Those girls weren't flirting with boys! They were chasing my boy, my baby! Why, those . . . those . . . hussies! How dare they? You little flirts! Get away from him! Do you hear me? Shoo! Go away!

Certainly my son would not respond to such immature antics.

But he was.

He was splashing them back, smiling and looking manly with his chest all puffed out and his hands on his hips. The summer wind was shamelessly at work, right before my eyes, enticing my boy into puberty. He shouldn't respond yet, should he? He's only eleven.

Eleven?

Eleven!

When did he turn eleven?

I shielded my eyes from the sun with my arm and continued to stare. I refused to blink. I didn't dare. I knew if I closed my eyes for even one second, my baby boy would suddenly be transformed into a man.

Mothers hold their children's hands
for a short while
but their hearts forever.

—Author Unknown

We will not hide these truths from our children;
we will tell the next generation
about the glorious deeds of the LORD,
about his power and his mighty wonders. . . .
He commanded our ancestors
to teach them to their children,
so the next generation might know them—
even the children not yet born—
and they in turn will teach their own children.
So each generation should set its hope anew on God,
not forgetting his glorious miracles
and obeying his commands.

PSALM 78:4-7, NLT

Fluffy Tea in the Tub

Once upon our anniversary we made plans for a getaway weekend. Everything went crazy at the last minute, and my husband called from work to say we had to cancel. We weren't escaping the bedlam in the morning after all. I was numb.

I could hear the neighbor boys yelling at my son in the backyard, so I sent them home. My son came inside and stepped on his sister's coloring book, and she threw crayons, so I sent them to their rooms. Then I sent myself to the couch, where I flopped on a gigantic mound of laundry, fresh from the dryer. I intended to have a good cry, but I was too sad or mad or tired or hopeless to squeeze out a single tear.

The doorbell rang. It was Wendy and Leslie, two college women from church.

Leslie headed for the bathroom, and Wendy said, "We heard."

I gave her my most pathetic expression and nodded.

"Where's your royal robe?"

"My what?"

"Your bathrobe. You have to take a bath. We're making dinner. Dale will be here in a few minutes to take your kids miniature golfing. Your husband will be home in an hour. Come. Your tub awaits, your majesty."

"But the laundry . . ."

"What laundry?" Wendy made a sweeping motion with her hand. "You have no laundry. You are the queen of anniversary bliss." She grabbed my robe from the heap and draped it over her arm.

"But the kids need . . ."

Wendy waved her hand again. "What kids? You have no children. You are a lady of leisure."

She escorted me down the hall and opened the bathroom door. Leslie grinned and stepped aside. Peach-scented bath bubbles gurgled in the tub. A dozen candles flickered like fireflies. Soothing classical music circled us.

"Now, go soak, your highness."

"Go soak my what?"

Wendy shook her head and left me alone in the midst of the loveliest pity party anyone had ever thrown for me. Not until I was completely submerged did I realize this was the first time in the five months we'd lived in this house that I had taken a real bath.

A tap sounded at the door, and Wendy entered carrying my silver tea tray. In twelve years of marriage I had never used it. Ever. She lowered the tray like a butler and offered me one of my own china teacups peaked with a swirl of whipped cream.

"What is this?"

"Fluffy Tea," she said. "I was going to make you some peppermint tea, but then I decided you needed my specialty. A good strong cup of Fluffy Tea. Try it."

She left, and I cautiously took a lick. Underneath the whipped cream was more whipped cream. The entire cup was nothing but whipped cream. Fluffy Tea!

Twenty minutes before, I was too dismal to even speak. Now I was up to my chin in peachy bubbles, sipping Fluffy Tea, which had come to me on a silver tray in a candlelit room where I miraculously had no laundry and no children.

Who says a weary mama's fairy tales don't come true?

Our anniversary dinner was delicious and memorable. Leslie's lemon chicken was pure bliss, served regally on china plates, and our wedding crystal goblets were each filled with sparkling water and a floating strawberry. My handsome prince held my hand across the table, and with great hope we made plans for what we would do on our next anniversary. And the one after that, and the one after that, until we lived happily ever after. (With the aid of an occasional cup of Fluffy Tea.)

The LORD is like a father to his children, tender and compassionate to those who fear him.

PSALM 103:13, NLT

A Mother's Prayer for Wisdom

Heavenly Father,

I am Your daughter. I am loved by You.

You know me by heart. You are always beside me. You know the bouts of anxiety and eagerness that have filled my life ever since I became a mother. You know what it's like to

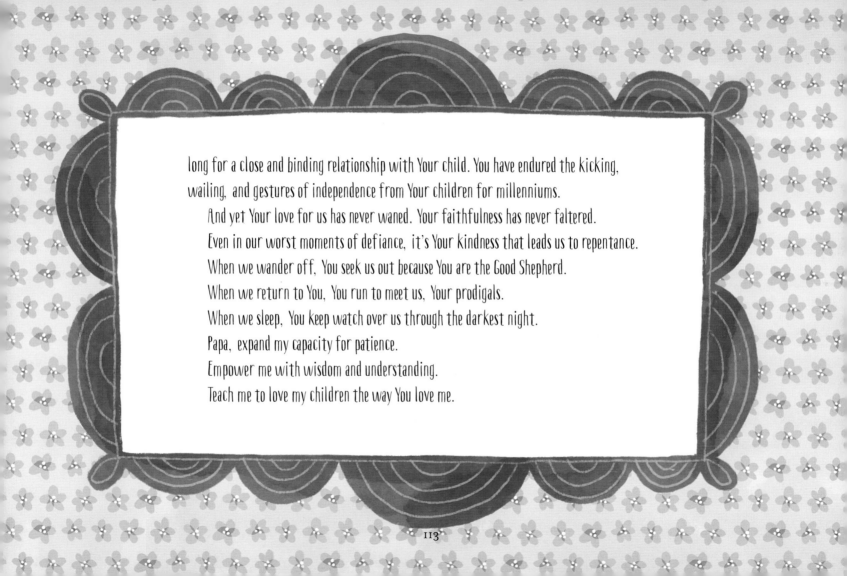

long for a close and binding relationship with Your child. You have endured the kicking, wailing, and gestures of independence from Your children for millenniums.

And yet Your love for us has never waned. Your faithfulness has never faltered.

Even in our worst moments of defiance, it's Your kindness that leads us to repentance.

When we wander off, You seek us out because You are the Good Shepherd.

When we return to You, You run to meet us, Your prodigals.

When we sleep, You keep watch over us through the darkest night.

Papa, expand my capacity for patience.

Empower me with wisdom and understanding.

Teach me to love my children the way You love me.

Love bears all things, believes all things, hopes all things, endures all things. Love never ends.

1 CORINTHIANS 13:7-8